Mind: The Original AI

AI: Ancient Intelligence

*Harness the original intelligence
you were born with.*

By
Thomas Lashan

Table of Contents

Foreword

We live in a time where artificial intelligence is transforming industries, economies, and daily life. Yet, while the world chases after external technologies, I believe we've overlooked the most extraordinary intelligence system of all, the one housed inside each of us.

Your mind isn't just a collection of thoughts and memories. It's an intricate, powerful program that runs your life, influences your decisions, and determines your outcomes. The difference between people who seem to move through life effortlessly and those who struggle often comes down to this: they've learned to work with their mind, not against it.

I wrote this book not as a motivational pep talk or a quick-fix guide but as a companion for those ready to reclaim their internal power. I want you to see your mind as the original AI, a living, breathing, learning system that, when consciously directed, can open doors you didn't even know existed.

I've experienced the highs and lows of this journey myself. I've battled habits, faced setbacks, fallen into the traps of old programs, and crawled out the other side. What I've learned is simple: *when you change the way you think, you change your world.*

This book is an invitation. An invitation to stop running outdated software written by past experiences, social conditioning, and fear, and to start programming your mind intentionally, with clarity, purpose, and belief.

You don't need another app, another hack, or another guru. You need to remember what you already have. And this book will show you how.

Welcome to your upgrade.

Introduction:
The Forgotten Power

There's something no one ever told us growing up: *your mind isn't you.*

It's a tool. A program. An operating system you've inherited, upgraded, and filled with instructions since the moment you were born.

The challenge is that most of us are still running outdated software.

Some of it was written by well-meaning parents, teachers, culture, and friends. Some of it came from pain, rejection, setbacks, and those moments no one else remembers but you can't seem to forget. And whether you realise it or not, these old programs are running silently in the background, influencing your thoughts, actions, and results.

But here's the truth: **your mind is programmable**.

It's the original AI, an intelligent system designed to serve you, not sabotage you. And once you understand how it works, you'll see how easy it is to clean out old files, install new patterns, and start operating at a higher frequency of peace, courage, and clarity.

I didn't arrive at this understanding by reading books alone. I arrived here through frustration. Through moments where nothing made sense and everything I touched turned to dust. Through nights staring at the ceiling, asking myself, *Why does this keep happening to me?*

And one day, the answer landed, **It wasn't happening to me. It was happening because of me.**

Not in a blame-yourself way, but in a liberating, powerful, *finally-take-the-wheel-of-your- own-life* kind of way.

That realisation was the start of everything. And this book, well, it's your start.

What you're about to read is a collection of truths, lived experiences, tested practices, and empowering perspectives that can shift your inner operating system and wake up the original AI within you.

If you're ready to stop living on autopilot…

If you're ready to stop being a passenger in your own story…

If you're ready to plug back into the universal energy you were always connected to…

Then let's begin.

Time to reboot.

We arrive in this world without a user manual, yet we spend a lifetime assembling ourselves like a complicated piece of furniture with missing instructions. If you've ever tried putting together a flat-pack wardrobe with only half the directions, you know how it feels to navigate life's complexities. This book aims to provide insights, not as a rulebook but as a toolkit, to help you build a life that feels authentic, purposeful, and uniquely yours.

"You have power over your mind, not outside events. Realise this, and you will find strength." — *Marcus Aurelius*

The mind is not just a biological organ; it's an energy-powered phenomenon, operating both consciously and unconsciously. Recognising this duality is crucial. You can either fight your mind, becoming your own worst enemy, or make it your greatest ally, aligning your thoughts and energy with your desired outcomes. I've learned, often the hard way, that life becomes infinitely more fulfilling when you choose the latter.

The Escalator Revelation

Let me share a simple but powerful moment that altered how I saw my relationship with my mind. You might have experienced this yourself: approaching a stopped escalator. You see it not moving. You tell yourself to treat it like stairs. Yet, as you step on, there's a strange wobble, a disorienting moment of imbalance. Why? Because your subconscious mind had already filed away an automatic program for "how to step onto an escalator" years ago.

Despite your conscious instruction, that old program kicked in.

This moment struck me like lightning; if my mind was running old programs for something so trivial, what else in my life was I being guided by without realising it?

Carl Jung once wrote, "Until you make the unconscious conscious, it will direct your life and you will call it fate."

Chapter 1:
Energy, Programs, and Emotional Signatures

Our minds are constantly spinning, like a hard drive sorting files and programs, some helpful, others outdated or corrupt. As we live, our experiences become emotional imprints, saved like files in our subconscious. Some of these are positive, fuelling our creativity and confidence. Others are like viruses, slowing down our mental processing, leading to hesitation, procrastination, or even self-sabotage.

You've likely noticed this: when you're energised, you make better choices. When you're depleted, life feels heavier. This isn't a coincidence, it's physics. Everything is energy, including thought. When we hold onto unresolved experiences or emotional baggage, it clutters our mental hard drive, slowing our decision-making and blocking new ideas from surfacing.

"Energy flows where attention goes." — *Tony Robbins*

The question isn't whether you have these files; we all do. The question is how you're going to manage, upgrade, and delete them.

Subconscious and Conscious Mind: The Constant Dialogue

Imagine your mind as a computer with two primary drives:

- **The Conscious Mind**: your active awareness, what you focus on in the moment.

- **The Subconscious Mind**: a vast archive of every experience, belief, and emotional response you've ever had.

When faced with a decision, say, a friend invites you to a movie, your conscious mind quickly consults your subconscious archive. Was your last movie experience good? Were you with people you enjoyed? How did the film make you feel? Based on this data, you'll decide.

But here's the kicker: negative experiences often leave deeper grooves in the subconscious than positive ones. This means that one bad memory can outweigh ten good ones. That's why people avoid love after heartbreak, or opportunities after failures.

"The mind is like a fertile garden in which anything that is planted, flowers or weeds, will grow." — *Bruce Lee*

The good news? You can consciously plant new seeds. Before we do, here is another look at the same information.

Your Mind's Operating System

Let's simplify this: think of your mind as a spinning wheel, always moving, always processing. The subconscious stores every moment you've lived, every emotion you've felt, and every belief you've adopted. The conscious mind acts like the search function on a computer: it taps into those files to help you make decisions.

Say a friend invites you to a party. Your conscious mind consults the subconscious: Was the last party a good experience? Was the food terrible? Did you laugh, cry, or feel bored? Based on that, you decide whether to accept to go along.

Now imagine how many of these micro-decisions happen every single day, hundreds, maybe thousands. Everyone leaves a trace in your subconscious. The good, the bad, the neutral.

Your mind stores incomplete files, too. That argument you left unresolved, that traumatic memory you never processed, that goal you gave up on halfway through, they're all still there. And like too many open tabs on a computer, they slow down your system.

This is why people feel stuck, overwhelmed, or perpetually exhausted. Not because life is inherently hard, but because their mental operating system is clogged.

"The mind is everything. What you think, you become."
— *Buddha*

Reprogramming the System

The good news? You can clean house. You can close those tabs. But you must consciously decide what stays and what goes, what is replaced.

In *Breaking the Habit of Being Yourself*, Dr. Joe Dispenza explains that 95% of our thoughts, actions, and emotions are run by subconscious programs. To change your life, you must first become aware of those programs. Then, through new habits and emotional conditioning, overwrite them.

And it begins with energy. If you've had disappointments, and you have, we all have, those moments leave programs in your subconscious. If you keep replaying them, they'll keep showing up in your present. You're not cursed; you're conditioned.

As the ancient wisdom goes: **"Where attention goes, energy flows."**

When Disappointment Becomes a Default Program

One of the most damaging viruses in this mental operating system is unprocessed disappointment. Left unchecked, it loops, infecting new experiences, causing us to react with doubt or fear. The brain, seeking efficiency, defaults to what it knows, and if what it knows is hurt, rejection, or failure, it will instinctively anticipate the same. The law of attraction gives you more of what you don't want; remember the ancient wisdom.

"You can't go back and change the beginning, but you can start where you are and change the ending." — *C.S. Lewis*

The secret is to interrupt these loops and install new, positive programs. It requires conscious effort, but the rewards are exponential.

Simple and Effective Daily Start

You hold the power to shape the energy of every day, and it all begins the moment you open your eyes. Your first thoughts set the tone not only for your own momentum but for everyone who looks to you for strength, direction, and inspiration. Choose, deliberately and boldly, to start your day with positive energy. Make it your anchor. Make it your fuel.

We cannot always control what the day brings, but we can control how we enter it. You have faced challenges, you have risen before, and you will rise again. That strength is inside you, and it's sparked each morning by the mindset you choose. He who starts with gratitude, optimism, and clarity will always lead you to have a better day, even through chaos.

My Awakening: Breaking the Smoking Loop

Before my escalator epiphany, life had already been nudging me toward awareness. I reached a point where everything felt stale. Days blurred together like an endless Groundhog Day. I decided, first step, to quit smoking and get healthy. Sounds simple. Except my environment didn't want me to change. Friends laughed, offering me cigarettes even after I'd vowed to quit. I failed. Several times. Each failure made it easier to justify the next; my mind confirmed that.

Then I came across a quote that hit me square in the face:

"If you always do what you've always done, you'll always get what you've always got."

— Henry Ford

I realised my environment was part of the problem. I needed to make a radical shift. So I left behind the friends who enabled my old habits. I changed my routine, joined a gym, and filled my days with people and places that aligned with the person I wanted to become. This can only happen by deciding to take the steps.

It wasn't just willpower. It was environment engineering. Because your habits are a product of your environment, and you cannot consistently outperform your surroundings.

Remembering thousands of thoughts are being produced.

James Clear, in his book *Atomic Habits*, writes, "Environment is the invisible hand that shapes human behaviour."

The Power of Small Wins

Change doesn't happen just through declarations. It happens through decisions—small, consistent wins.

If you want to transform your health, your finances, and your mindset, start with one conscious decision at a time. Replace the chocolate bar with a glass of water. Go for a ten-minute walk. Meditate for five minutes. Every choice towards change is confirmation for the person you're becoming.

And the mind, loyal to efficiency, will soon automate those new programs. You will soon have good habits that support your daily positive changes.

As Tony Robbins says, **"It's not what we do once in a while that shapes our lives. It's what we do consistently."**

Success isn't built on monumental overnight changes. It's constructed brick by brick, through small, deliberate wins. The mind learns through repetition and reward. One conscious choice not to grab a soft drink, one decision to take a walk instead of sulk, begins a chain reaction. Remind yourself that bad, unhealthy decisions will have detrimental effects on your health.

Give yourself visible reminders. Post-it notes. A new haircut. An app notification reminding you of your new path. I even tied a string around my wrist once as a physical anchor to my intention. It worked.

Positive Energy Isn't Optional — It's Essential

Same problem. Two reactions: anger and defeatism, or curiosity and optimism. Which one moves you forward?

Negative emotions drain physical and mental energy; giving up then becomes easy. Positivity looks towards change, being happy with change replenishes, which makes you want more. You don't need to pretend life is perfect, just accept it to be ongoing, and that you have power over your attitude.

"Between stimulus and response, there is a space. In that space is our power to choose our response." — *Viktor Frankl*

There's a universal energy always moving forward. Whether you're aligned with it or not, it's expanding as it moves. Your job is to catch up, to merge your energy with it. Think of it like opening an app on your phone; you have to actively tap in.

Slow down. Take a breath. Decide what you want to tune into for better flow.

Harnessing the Source: Conscious Energy Selection

Think of your awareness as a store. You get to choose which programs to shop for. Fear? Doubt? Joy? Courage? All available at any moment.

To improve your decision-making and emotional resilience:

14

- Slow down to introduce awareness of your power.

- Spend that time doing what nourishes you, and tap into good energy.

- Walk. Meditate. Garden. Read. Exercise.

- Breathing deeply through your nose to calm your system.

The better you get at this, the clearer your mind becomes, and the faster your decisions align with your highest potential, giving you the power to enjoy your process.

Habits: Reprogramming the Operating System

Habits are efficiency programs. The mind loves them because they free up decision-making space. Unfortunately, it doesn't distinguish between good and bad. Eat junk food daily? It installs that. Exercise daily? It installs that too. This knowledge will give you the power to start working on some good habits.

The secret is conscious replacement, not suppression; ignoring does not make it go away. New habits overwrite old ones through consistent choices, remember repeated positive action is an energising feeling that moves you forward for more.

Your future isn't predetermined by fate, it's determined by the choices you made, and are making. It's shaped by the tiny, seemingly insignificant choices you make. The old files are there, which is influencing what's next, but you can decide what to open, how to respond to it, what to delete, and what to rewrite.

The mind is both the battlefield and the weapon. Make it your greatest ally. You can have peace in a chaotic day, or chaos in a peaceful day, you choose.

The Phantom Vibrate — Another Example of the Spinning Wheel at Work

Earlier in this book, we spoke about the mind's spinning wheel, how our subconscious holds programs, unresolved thoughts, and past experiences, constantly cycling until something triggers them to surface. Now, here's another example you'll instantly relate to.

Have you ever had your phone on silent and felt a phantom vibration? That faint buzz you swear happened, only to check your phone and find nothing there. It happens to nearly all of us. Why? Because we've programmed ourselves to anticipate that sensation. We've built a subconscious loop: waiting for a call, a message, a notification. That anticipation becomes a subtle, invisible program running in the background, and sometimes the spinning wheel of your mind lands on it, even when no external event has occurred.

This is harmless in the case of a phantom phone vibrate. But what about the other loops? The ones loaded with self-doubt, old disappointments, or unchecked negative beliefs? The ones you aren't even conscious of, but that randomly surface, making you question yourself, feel anxious, or hesitate in moments that matter.

Just like the phantom vibrate makes you instinctively check your phone, these old programs cause you to react in ways you may not even understand, unless you become aware that it's happening.

The lesson here is simple: if you can catch the phantom vibrate, you can catch these subconscious thought loops too. Awareness is your tool. Every time a self-defeating or outdated thought surfaces, treat it like that rogue vibration. Acknowledge it, recognise it for what it is, just a programmed reflex, and choose to let it go or replace it with something better.

This small but powerful awareness practice is how we begin rewiring and strengthening our internal AI.

Chapter 2:
The Labels You Wear

From the moment we're born, the world starts sticking labels on us like price tags at a clearance sale.

"He's shy."

"She's bossy." "They're difficult." "You're a good boy." "You're trouble."

Some of them you wear proudly for a while. Others feel like an ill-fitting jacket you were forced to carry through life. And before long, those labels don't just describe you, they start to *define* you.

Carl Jung nailed it when he said:

"The world will ask you who you are, and if you do not know, the world will tell you."

I realised this one night in my twenties, sitting alone in my car after another failed relationship, a business deal falling apart, and friends drifting away. I looked in the rearview mirror and thought, *"Who even am I now?"*

That question can feel like a crisis, but it's actually an invitation.

"The moment we truly identify with a problem, when we stop avoiding it and allow ourselves to own it, the mind begins to work in our favour. It's one of the most powerful tools we have, constantly searching for solutions the moment we shift from resistance to acceptance. Every obstacle, every sticking point, every setback holds within it the seed of its own solution. When we align ourselves with the reality of our circumstances rather than fight against them, clarity begins to surface, creative answers emerge, and better outcomes naturally follow. The key is in the alignment: problems persist when we disown them, but they unravel when we step fully into them."

Identity Is a Story You Keep Telling Yourself

Your identity isn't your job title, your relationship status, or the postcode you grew up in. It's the collection of stories you've chosen to believe about yourself.

Some were written by you. Most were written by others.

And the problem is, we rarely stop to question who authored them in the first place.

Maybe you were told you weren't academic, so you carried *"not smart enough"* into adulthood like an invisible weight.

Maybe you failed at something early, and the label *"I'm a screw-up"* clung to you. Or perhaps you've always been the peacemaker, the joker, the reliable one, and it's exhausting, but it feels safer than confronting who you'd be without that role.

James Clear talks about this elegantly:

"True behavior change is identity change. You might start a habit because of motivation, but you'll only stick with it because it becomes part of your identity."

Which means if you want to change your life, you don't just change your habits, you change what you believe about who you are.

The Mask I Didn't Know I Was Wearing

I'll share something raw with you.

For years, I wore the mask of *"I've got this."* The guy who never needed help. The one who handled everything, made the tough calls, brushed it off, and stayed cool. I wore it so well, I even believed it. But underneath was a kid who was terrified of being a disappointment.

That fear made me overwork, over-promise, and over-give until I burned out. And when that mask started to slip, I didn't know who I was without it.

The truth is, most people are walking around wearing masks they didn't choose.

And the wild thing? The world rewards those masks. It praises your overachiever mask, loves your party-animal mask, and depends on your responsible older sibling mask.

But deep down, you know when a mask stops fitting.

Unlearning the Lies

Before you can build a new identity, you have to unlearn the lies. Write this down somewhere:

"I am not my past. I am not my mistakes. I am not the labels others gave me. I am not the worst thing I've done. I am not the version of me who made survival-based decisions in hard seasons."

You were doing the best you could with what you knew at the time.

The goal now isn't to erase the past, it's to reclaim authorship of the story.

Your Identity Is Fluid — And That's a Good Thing

We've been sold this idea that you need to "find yourself" like you're some ancient artefact buried under years of rubble.

But you're not lost. You're evolving. Carl Jung once said:

"We cannot change anything until we accept it. Condemnation does not liberate, it oppresses."

Meaning, you can't shame yourself into growth. You outgrow old identities when you stop condemning them and start getting curious.

Why did I believe I was bad with money?

Why did I stay in relationships that diminished me?

Why did I think I had to prove my worth by overachieving?

21

The answers will shock you. And they'll free you.

The Pivot: Choose New Labels

You get to choose who you are becoming.

Pick labels that serve your next chapter. Write them down. Say them out loud. Move like you already are them.

I am disciplined.

I am a person who keeps my word.

I am becoming stronger, clearer, braver every single day.

I am someone who speaks up, Who walks away from what insults my soul, Who builds things worth building.

Even if it feels fake at first. Especially if it does.

Because identity change feels awkward before it feels authentic.

The Energy Shift

Here's what happens when you start claiming new labels; your energy changes. People feel it. Some will be drawn to it. Others will resist it because your growth threatens their comfort zone.

And that's okay.

Not everyone gets to come with you. Not every relationship belongs in your next season.

I call this *energetic alignment.* When who you are internally starts matching what you're putting into the world.

It's intoxicating. It's magnetic. It's what you were born for.

Coming Next: Reprogramming the Inner Dialogue

Now that you've cracked open your identity, it's time to tackle the inner conversation running 24/7 in your head.

The one narrating your worth. The one negotiating your limits.

The one deciding whether you're capable or not.

We'll unpack how to reprogram that voice, install new beliefs, and claim new standards, so your external world can finally catch up to your internal vision.

And trust me, this is where the real game begins.

Chapter 3:
Reprogramming the
Inner Dialogue

There's a voice in your head.

It's there when you wake up. It's there when you screw up.

It's there when you win, too, though you'll notice it often speaks louder during your losses.

And here's the uncomfortable truth:

Most people spend their entire lives being bullied by their own inner voice.

That voice isn't just commenting on your life, it's shaping it. As Napoleon Hill said in *Think and Grow Rich*:

"You are the master of your fate, the captain of your soul, because you have the power to control your thoughts."

But the problem is, no one teaches us *how*.

The Invisible Narrator

Imagine for a moment that your inner voice was an actual person. Let's call him the Narrator.

Now, picture if, from the moment you woke up, this Narrator followed you around, saying things like:

"You always leave things too late." "You'll never pull this off."

"People like you don't get those opportunities."

How long before you told him to shut up and get out of your house?

Yet we let that Narrator live rent-free in our heads for decades, no questions asked. Why?

Because most of those internal scripts were installed when you were too young to fight back.

A careless comment from a teacher.

A rejection from someone you admired. A string of failures you never processed.

Those old dialogues calcify into beliefs, and those beliefs quietly write the script of your life.

Awareness Is the First Power Move

You can't upgrade what you're unaware of. The first step is noticing the pattern.

Next time you hesitate, sabotage yourself, or feel yourself shrinking, stop and ask:

"What did I just tell myself in that moment?"

I've caught myself saying things like:

"You're not smart enough for this room."

"Don't get your hopes up, you'll just get let down." "People probably don't take you seriously."

None of those are facts.

They're inherited, outdated programming.

And here's the liberating thing:

If you can identify the thought, you can interrupt it. If you can interrupt it, you can rewire it.

Interrupt. Replace. Reinforce.

Reprogramming your inner dialogue isn't about blind positivity. It's about creating a new, empowering internal baseline.

The framework is simple:

1.   Interrupt the thought.

Notice it. Call it out.

"Ah, there's that old 'not good enough' story again."

2.   Replace it immediately.

Drop in a new statement, one rooted in truth, or one you choose to believe now.

"I'm learning. I'm adapting. I'm worthy of being in this room."

Even if you don't fully believe it yet. Especially if you don't.

3.   Reinforce it consistently.

The brain works on repetition.

Neural pathways deepen the more you fire them.

That means every time you say the new line, you're literally reshaping the architecture of your mind.

This is neuroscience, not fluff.

As Dr. Joe Dispenza explains:

"Nerve cells that fire together, wire together."

Meaning, the more you practice a thought, the more automatic it becomes.

Write Your New Script

Here's an exercise that changed everything for me. And I'll be real, it felt awkward at first.

But so does anything you've been conditioned to avoid.

Grab a notebook and write down five negative beliefs you regularly think about yourself.

Be honest. The ones you'd never say out loud.

Then, for each one, write the opposite, a belief that serves the person you're becoming.

Example:

❌ *"I always screw things up."*

☑️ *"I am resourceful. I recover fast and turn setbacks into setups."*

❌ *"People don't take me seriously."*

☑️ *"My presence carries weight. My voice matters in every room I enter."*

❌ *"I'll probably fail again."*

☑️ *"Every attempt sharpens me. I get better, stronger, clearer each time."*

Now say them out loud. Daily. Morning and night.

Out loud.

Yes — out loud.

Why?

Because the subconscious responds more strongly to what it hears in your own voice. This isn't a cute self-help trick—It's how the human brain gets reconditioned.

The Shift You'll Start to Feel

After a while, you'll catch yourself mid-thought.

A negative voice will start, and before it can land, a new, empowered thought will interrupt it.

Where you used to spiral, you'll redirect. Where you used to freeze, you'll act.

Where you used to settle, you'll raise your standards.

And you'll feel different, not in a superficial, fake-positive way, but in a steady, quiet, unshakable way.

That's the feeling of coming home to yourself.

Next: Claiming Your Standards and Boundaries

Now that you've begun rewriting the internal script, it's time to draw the external lines. The world treats you how you teach it to.

In the next chapter, we'll unpack how to claim your standards, set unbreakable boundaries, and stop tolerating what shrinks you.

Because the version of you you're becoming demands a new set of rules. And you're the one who gets to write them.

Chapter 4:
Claiming Your Standards and Boundaries

Let's be blunt:

You don't get what you deserve in life. You get what you tolerate.

I know that's a confronting line, but it's one that changed my life the first time I heard it. Because it forced me to ask a question most people avoid:

"What have I been tolerating that's keeping me small?"

We all have a list. Jobs that drain us. People who drain us.

Habits that dull our edge.

Conversations we know we shouldn't still be having. Environments that don't match our vision.

And here's the kicker: you'll never outperform your standards.

Your life, your business, your relationships, they rise or fall to meet the level you decide is *acceptable*.

Raise your standards, and your life recalibrates to meet them.

Drop your standards, and the world will happily step over them.

The Silent Contracts You Don't Realise You're Making

Most people are walking around with invisible, unspoken agreements they never consciously chose.

Like:

- *"I'll keep tolerating this relationship because being alone feels scarier than being unhappy."*

- *"I'll accept being underpaid because I don't want to rock the boat."*

- *"I'll keep shrinking my ideas because I don't want to make other people uncomfortable."*

Those are silent contracts.

And every day you don't tear them up, you reinforce them.

You don't rise to your goals — you fall to your standards.

Drawing the Line

A powerful, pivotal moment in my life came the day I realised:

If I want different outcomes, I have to demand a different standard from myself and everything around me.

That meant having uncomfortable conversations.

It meant walking away from deals and people that no longer fit.

It meant raising my expectations of how I'd show up in the world, even when no one was watching.

And that's where boundaries come in.

Not as walls to keep the world out, but as gates that protect what matters most. Boundaries aren't about other people.

They're about you deciding what gets access to your time, your energy, your heart, your creativity, and your future.

How to Set Unbreakable Boundaries Without Guilt

I used to think setting boundaries meant conflict.

I associated it with tension, confrontation, and awkward moments.

But what I've learned is that being *clear is kind*.

When you set clean, non-negotiable boundaries, three things happen:

1. You regain control of your energy.

No more leaking power into situations that drain you.

2. People respect you more.

Even the ones who resist at first, because strength commands respect.

3.   You create space for what actually aligns with your vision.

The things you've been chasing can't land while your life is filled with noise and clutter.

And here's the best part: you don't have to explain or justify your boundaries.

"No is a complete sentence."

If it costs you your peace, it's too expensive.

The Standards Audit

Right now, you've got standards in every area of your life, whether you're aware of them or not.

A quick exercise:

Take five minutes and write down your current standards in these areas:

- Health & energy

- Finances & wealth creation

- Relationships & friendships

- Business & career

- Personal growth

- Environments you spend time in

Be brutally honest.

Then ask yourself: **"If I lived at this standard for the next 10 years, would I be proud of where it takes me?"**

If the answer is no, raise the standard. Today.

Not in theory. Not next year. Now.

And remember:

The gap between where you are and where you want to be isn't discipline. It's standards.

The Power of Deciding

One of the most underrated, life-altering powers you have is the ability to *decide*. Not to 'try'.

Not to 'hope'.

Not to 'wait and see'.

To decide.

And when you truly decide on a new standard, when you draw a line in the sand and say, *"I don't live below this anymore"* —the universe rearranges itself around that energy.

Opportunities start showing up. The wrong people fall away.

Your confidence grows because self-respect is built in the moments you refuse to negotiate with your lesser self.

As Tony Robbins said:

"In any moment of decision, the best thing you can do is the right thing. The next best thing is the wrong thing. The worst thing you can do is nothing."

Next: Reclaiming Your Relationship with Fear

Now that you've drawn your lines and raised your standards, there's one more thing we need to address: fear.

Not to get rid of it, but to master your relationship with it.

Because the life you want exists on the other side of the things you're currently avoiding.

In the next chapter, we'll dismantle fear's illusions, redefine what it means to be brave, and give you the tools to step into discomfort without losing your nerve.

Ready to walk through the fire? Let's go.

Chapter 5:
A Deeper Delve Into Us

We often talk about artificial intelligence as though it's something separate from us, a technology, a tool, an external force advancing at breathtaking speed. But the truth is, we've always had our own version of AI within us. The human mind is the original intelligent operating system. The way it gathers data, stores memories, learns patterns, predicts outcomes, and makes decisions is no different from how artificial intelligence is designed to function.

The challenge isn't whether we have this intelligence, it's whether we *trust it*. Too often, we've allowed fear, conditioning, and limited beliefs to suppress our innate abilities. But when we increase our confidence, sharpen our knowledge, and become conscious of our internal resources, our subconscious, our intuition, and our learned wisdom, we become exponentially more powerful. Pair this with the external resources at our fingertips, search engines, books, mentors, and the wealth of human knowledge, and we can operate with the efficiency and clarity of any AI.

The Powers We Were Born With

Each of us arrives in this world carrying untapped, undeniable powers, love, peace, courage, happiness, and truth. These aren't traits we acquire later in life; they're part of our original design. They exist within us at birth, untainted and absolute. As children, we live from these qualities effortlessly. We don't question whether we are worthy of love, whether we can be happy, or if we're brave enough to try something new. It simply is. We exist in a natural state of curiosity, trust, and joy.

But life, in all its unpredictability, slowly begins to chip away at these inner powers. Each experience, every moment of pain, disappointment, and fear, subtly erodes the purity of these qualities. And unless we consciously reclaim them, we risk forgetting who we truly are.

How It Happens: A Simple Example

Consider this: imagine a child, lost in a world of playful adventure, bouncing on the couch without a care in the world. In those moments, they're embodying courage, happiness, and peace. Then, one split-second decision, a leap off the couch, goes horribly wrong. Pain shoots through their body, tears follow, and in that very moment, something profound happens. The unshaken confidence to act without fear begins to crack. Pain introduces fear. The happiness of play is replaced by sadness. The peace of the moment turns into internal chaos.

And while it might seem like a small, insignificant childhood memory, it's moments like these, repeated in different forms over the years, that slowly condition us. We begin to associate risk with danger, expression with rejection, and vulnerability with pain. Bit by bit, our natural powers of love, peace, courage, happiness, and truth get buried beneath layers of learned protection mechanisms.

The Shift to a Negative Operating System

As these layers build, we unknowingly start operating from their opposites:

Love becomes hate or apathy. Peace turns into inner chaos. Courage is replaced by fear. Happiness fades into sadness.

Truth gets hidden beneath lies, often lies we tell ourselves.

This is how we lose ourselves, not in dramatic events, but in subtle, cumulative moments that reshape our inner world.

Reclaiming the Powers Within

The first step in reclaiming those powers is to recognise what's happened. To pause and reflect on the ways life has conditioned us to shrink. The truth is, those original powers never left us; they've simply been buried under the weight of unhealed experiences and misguided beliefs.

The work now is to identify where in our lives we're operating from fear, chaos, sadness, hate, or dishonesty, and to actively shift back toward the higher qualities we were born with.

Ask yourself:

Where have I allowed fear to replace my courage? Where has sadness silenced my happiness?

Where has chaos unsettled my peace?

Where have lies, even small ones, eroded my truth?

Where has love been traded for resentment or indifference?

When you become conscious of this, you reclaim the power to choose differently. And with each new choice, you begin to reinstall your positive internal operating system.

A New Operating System

The goal isn't to avoid pain or failure; those are inevitable parts of life. The goal is to learn how to feel it, heal it, and stay connected to your true nature. To operate from a foundation of love, peace, courage, happiness, and truth, no matter what life throws your way. Because that's who you truly are underneath the noise.

When you do this, you stop living life at the mercy of external circumstances and begin creating from within. And from that place, anything becomes possible.

Chapter 6:
The Mind as a Garden

The Seeds We Sow

If the powers we were born with are like sunlight and fresh soil, then our thoughts are the seeds we plant in that garden. Every day, with every thought, belief, and feeling, we're planting something. The challenge is that most of us inherited seeds we didn't choose. Seeds of limitation, self-doubt, fear, unworthiness, passed down through generations, social conditioning, and our own unexamined experiences.

As children, we absorbed these messages without question:

Be careful, you might get hurt. Don't get your hopes up.

You're not smart enough for that. Life's a struggle, better get used to it.

Each message, whether spoken or implied, planted something in the fertile ground of our minds. And without conscious awareness, those seeds took root, grew, and started to shape the way we saw ourselves and the world.

What We Focus On, Grows

The mind is a powerful and obedient servant. It doesn't judge whether a thought is good or bad, true or false; it simply nurtures whatever you consistently feed it. Focus on fear, and fear will multiply. Dwell on limitations, and you'll find them at every turn. But when you learn to focus on courage, peace, love, and gratitude, you begin to shift the soil itself.

This isn't about false positivity. It's not pretending pain or struggle don't exist. It's about choosing which thoughts you give your energy to. Recognising that while you may not control every event in your life, you always control how you respond to it, and that response will either plant weeds or wildflowers.

The Inner Dialogue

Most people live at the mercy of a constant, unconscious inner dialogue. A running commentary that reinforces their fears and limitations:

I can't do that. I'll never be good enough. What's the point in trying?

This always happens to me.

And the more you entertain these thoughts, the deeper they dig into your subconscious, eventually becoming beliefs. And beliefs are powerful, because they quietly dictate your decisions, your actions, and ultimately, your reality.

Changing the Conversation

The way out isn't to fight the old thoughts, it's to start planting new ones. To interrupt the unconscious narrative with conscious, empowered statements:

I am capable. I can learn this. I've overcome before, and I will again. I am worthy of love, success, and peace.

At first, this might feel awkward or even false. That's normal. You're reconditioning a mind that's been running old scripts for years, sometimes decades. But every time you catch yourself slipping into an old, limiting thought and choose a new one, you weaken the old pattern. And over time, the new pattern takes hold.

Emotion: The Water to Your Seeds

Thought alone isn't enough. Emotion is what gives thoughts their power. A thought repeated without emotion is like a seed thrown on dry soil; it won't take root. But when you attach a feeling, excitement, gratitude, or determination, that thought gains momentum.

This is why it's so important to cultivate positive emotional states. Not in a performative way, but in an authentic, grounded way. Gratitude for small things. Courage in small acts. Joy in simple moments. These emotional states water the seeds of better thoughts, and before long, a new inner landscape begins to take shape.

Your Garden, Your Responsibility

No one can do this work for you. Just like no one can exercise for you or breathe for you, no one else can tend to the garden of your mind. But when you commit to this, everything changes. Challenges still come, but you handle them differently. Doubts still whisper, but you don't give them power. And slowly, you reclaim the beautiful, fertile, and powerful inner world you were always meant to live in.

Key Takeaway:

The thoughts you choose and the emotions you attach to them are shaping your life in every moment. Choose wisely. Plant consciously. Water generously.

Chapter 7:
The Power of Thought

Our thoughts shape our reality. They influence our emotions, actions, and ultimately, our identity. By understanding the thought process, we can recognise how repetitive thinking patterns form habits, which in turn define our personality.

Key Concepts:

- **Thoughts as Energy:** Every thought emits energy, influencing our internal state and external interactions.

- **The Thought Cycle:**

    o **Think:** Initiate a thought.

    o **Feel:** Experience an emotion linked to the thought.

    o **Act:** Behave based on the emotion.

    o **Become:** Solidify this pattern into a habit, shaping identity

- **Mindfulness:** Being aware of our thoughts allows us to guide them positively, fostering a healthier mindset.

Breaking the Habit Loop

Habits are behaviours formed through repetition. They can be beneficial or detrimental. Understanding how they form empowers us to change them.

Habit Formation Process:

1. **Cue:** A trigger that initiates the behaviour.

2. **Routine:** The behaviour itself.

3. **Reward:** The benefit gained, reinforcing the habit.

Strategies for Change:

- **Identify Triggers:** Recognise what prompts the habit.

- **Replace Routines:** Substitute negative behaviours with positive ones.

- **Set Clear Goals:** Define what you want to achieve.

- **Strengthen Willpower:** Build resilience to resist old patterns

Personal Insight:

Changing habits requires patience and persistence. It's about making conscious choices daily to align actions with desired outcomes.

Embracing Unlimited Thinking

Our beliefs and past experiences can limit our potential. By challenging these limitations, we open ourselves to growth and fulfilment.

Understanding Limitations:

- **External Influences:** Media, culture, and upbringing shape our beliefs.

- **Self-Imposed Barriers:** Fear, doubt, and past failures can hinder progress.

Path to Empowerment:

- **Self-Reflection:** Examine and question existing beliefs.

- **Affirmation:** Reinforce positive self-identity.

- **Visualisation:** Imagine achieving goals to motivate action.

- **Equality Mindset:** See others without prejudice, fostering empathy and understanding.

Core Message:

You have the power to redefine your narrative. By embracing change and letting go of limiting beliefs, you can lead a life of purpose and joy.

Final Reflection:

Transformation begins with a single thought. By understanding the interplay between thoughts, habits, and beliefs, you can take control of your life. Embrace the journey of self-discovery, and remember: the mind is a powerful tool—use it wisely.

Chapter 8:
Recognising Patterns and
Breaking Cycles

The Echo of the Past

If you pay close attention to your life, the situations you find yourself in, the relationships you attract, and the problems you seem to keep facing, you'll notice a pattern. It might be subtle, or it might be glaringly obvious, but it's there. Life has a way of circling us back to the same lessons until we finally learn them.

This isn't bad luck or coincidence. It's life giving you opportunities to evolve. Every pattern you experience is a reflection of what's happening inside you, a mirror held up to your subconscious beliefs.

Why Patterns Repeat

The subconscious mind, once programmed, will run the same loops over and over because it craves familiarity. Even if that familiarity is uncomfortable or destructive, it's known, and the unknown terrifies the unconscious mind.

That's why people stay in unhealthy relationships, repeat financial struggles, or sabotage opportunities. It's not that they consciously choose pain — it's that their inner operating system is wired for it, and they haven't yet interrupted the cycle.

Identifying Your Patterns

The first step in breaking any cycle is awareness. You can't fix what you won't face. Take an honest inventory of your life:

What problems keep showing up in different forms? What kind of people do you keep attracting?

Where do you feel stuck, no matter how hard you try?

What beliefs are you holding about yourself that might be fuelling these outcomes?

This exercise isn't about blame or shame. It's about shining a light on the unconscious patterns driving your behaviour so you can finally choose differently.

The Power of Recognition

When you recognise a pattern, you weaken its hold. Awareness gives you the space between stimulus and response, the opportunity to pause and ask, "Is this who I still want to be? Is this the outcome I still want to create?"

For example:

You notice you always pull away when relationships get too close.

You realise you sabotage financial wins by overspending or

49

procrastinating. You catch yourself reacting with anger instead of curiosity when challenged.

These moments of recognition are gold. They're not signs of failure; they're signals that you're waking up.

Breaking the Cycle

Patterns are like well-worn tracks in the brain. The more you travel them, the deeper they get. Breaking them requires conscious effort to step off the old track and forge a new one.

Start small:

When the familiar thought arrives, pause. When the old reaction rises, breathe.

When the same type of situation appears, respond differently.

It might feel unnatural at first, even uncomfortable. That's the point. Growth always happens at the edge of discomfort. Every time you choose differently, you're weakening the old neural pathway and creating a new one.

Replacing Old with New

It's not enough to just stop the old behaviour; you must replace it with something empowering.

If you've operated from fear, start acting from courage.

If you've been reactive, practice curiosity.

If you've believed you're unworthy, remind yourself daily of your inherent value.

Over time, these new choices become habits. The new habits form new beliefs, and the new beliefs create a new reality.

Healing Through Action

Remember, you don't need to have all the answers to start. Clarity comes from action. Life isn't waiting for you to be perfect; it's waiting for you to be willing. Willing to try, to fail, to reflect, and to try again.

Each small interruption of a pattern is a win. Each moment of awareness is progress. This is how real, lasting change happens, not in giant leaps, but in daily, conscious, deliberate choices to be a little better, a little braver, a little wiser.

Key Takeaway:

Life will keep bringing you the same lessons until you learn them. Recognise the patterns, interrupt the cycles, and choose to create a new, empowered path forward.

Chapter 9:
The Power of Identity
and Attraction

Who You Believe You Are Is Who You Become

At the core of every decision you make, every habit you hold, and every circumstance you find yourself in is a single, powerful force: your identity. Not the identity others gave you, or the one society suggests you should wear, but the one you've accepted deep within.

If you believe you're unlucky, guess what you attract? Misfortune.

If you see yourself as someone people take advantage of, you'll find people to prove you right.

If you've told yourself you're bad with money, you'll unconsciously sabotage every opportunity for wealth.

Your subconscious is like a loyal servant, working day and night to confirm whatever identity you hold. And it does this by filtering your perceptions, choices, and actions in line with what you believe to be true.

The Law of Attraction — More Than a Concept

Most people misunderstand the Law of Attraction. It isn't about sitting on a couch, visualising cheques in the mail while doing nothing. It's about understanding that your dominant thoughts, emotions, and beliefs radiate an energetic frequency. And because like attracts like, you'll draw into your life people, opportunities, and experiences that match your internal state.

If your dominant thoughts are fear, lack, and self-doubt, your reality will mirror that. If your inner world is one of faith, gratitude, and abundance, life responds accordingly. **You Attract What You Are, Not What You Want**

This is one of the most misunderstood truths in personal development:

You can desire success, love, or peace all you like. But if your identity is one of lack, unworthiness, or limitation, you'll keep manifesting experiences that reflect those deeper beliefs.

That's why you must start with being, not just wanting.

Be courageous. Be abundant in your thinking. Be grateful, even before the evidence appears. Be the type of person your goals belong to.

Changing the Frequency

When you begin recognising old patterns (as we covered in Chapter Seven), you gain the power to shift your internal frequency. And when your inner world changes, your outer world must follow, not by magic, but by the natural laws of energy, attention, and action.

It's like tuning a radio. If you want to hear a different station, you don't beg the station to change its broadcast; you adjust your receiver. In life, your receiver is your subconscious mind, your beliefs, and your sense of identity.

Chapter 10:
Practical Laws of Attraction in Action

Let's demystify it and make it practical:

Clarity, get crystal clear on what you want, but more importantly, on who you must become to have it.

Embody the Feeling, act as though it's already yours. Not in a delusional way, but in how you carry yourself, speak, think, and decide.

Interrupt Old Patterns when limiting thoughts arise, and replace them immediately. As Napoleon Hill said, "You become what you think about most of the time."

Gratitude Amplifies Attraction: Be deeply thankful for what you already have. Gratitude multiplies whatever you focus it upon.

Take Inspired Action, attraction without action is delusion. Move boldly towards what you want. Life meets you halfway.

Rewriting the Internal Script

If identity drives outcomes and attraction mirrors your identity, then it makes sense to reprogram your internal narrative. Start small:

Change "I've always been bad with money" to "I'm learning to manage wealth wisely." Shift "I never meet the right people" to "I attract empowering, supportive relationships." Replace "I can't change" with "Every day I evolve into my best self."

Every thought is a seed. Plant enough of the right seeds, and a new garden grows.

Life Responds to Certainty

When you step into a new identity with certainty, life takes notice. The universe, or whatever you choose to call it, isn't responding to your hopes; it's responding to your belief. The Law of Attraction rewards conviction, not tentative wishing.

Final Word on Identity and Attraction

You're not here to simply wish for a better life. You're here to create it, consciously. Every thought, every belief, every action is shaping your future right now.

Your identity is the soil. Your thoughts are the seeds.

Your actions are the tending hands. Your reality is the harvest.

If you don't like what you're harvesting, don't curse the fruit; change the soil, plant new seeds, and water them daily with disciplined action and belief.

Key Takeaway:

The world you live in is a mirror of who you believe you are. Change your identity, shift your beliefs, and take aligned action, and your reality must respond in kind.

Chapter 11:
Creating a Personal Operating System — Designing a Life by Choice, Not Chance

You're Already Running a Program

Most people don't realise it, but every day they're running a personal operating system, a mental, emotional, and behavioural software that dictates how they perceive life, how they react, and ultimately, what they experience. The problem is, most of these systems were installed by accident.

Family. School. Society. Fear. Failure.

Successes that came too easily, or wounds that cut too deep.

Without realising, you picked up habits, beliefs, and identities not because you chose them, but because life presented them, and you accepted them as truth.

The Good News:

If your life is the product of an old operating system, you can upgrade it. You can design it. And when you do, everything changes.

Why Operating Systems Matter

Think about a computer. The hardware might be top shelf, but if the operating system is slow, outdated, or riddled with bugs, the machine underperforms. Life's the same.

You might have natural intelligence, creativity, or potential, but if your internal OS is based on fear, scarcity, and limitation, your outcomes will always be capped.

Change the system, and the performance shifts.

What's In Your Operating System?

Your personal operating system consists of:

- **Beliefs**: What you believe is possible, impossible, deserved, or out of reach.

- **Values**: What you hold as most important, even unconsciously.

- **Habits**: The small, daily rituals and behaviours that either build or break you.

- **Identity**: Who you fundamentally believe you are.

The dangerous part is that most of this is running silently in the background, which is why awareness is the first step.

How to Audit Your Current System

Before you can install a new one, you need to see what's currently running. Ask yourself:

- What do I believe about money, love, health, and success?

- Are my current habits taking me closer or further from the life I want?

- When I'm challenged, what is my automatic reaction? Courage or avoidance?

- Is my identity aligned with the person I want to be, or the person I settled for? Be ruthlessly honest. The truth might sting, but it also sets you free.

Designing Your New Operating System

Here's the beauty: you can write new code. The human brain is plastic, adaptive, and always listening. Every thought, every repeated behaviour, is a line of new code in your personal software.

Start here:

1. Clarify Who You Want to Become

Not just what you want to have, but who you want to *be*. Rich people who still feel poor on the inside find ways to lose their wealth. People who don't believe they deserve love sabotage good relationships. Identity drives outcomes.

Write it down:

"I am the type of person who..."

Example:

- I am the type of person who follows through.

- I am the type of person who prioritises my health.

- I am the type of person who adds value wherever I go.

2. Create Daily Identity Reinforcements

Your brain believes what it hears most. So feed it deliberately:

- Morning affirmations

- Journaling victories (even small ones)

- Surrounding yourself with people who reflect the identity you want to own.

3. Install New Habits That Align With the Identity

Big change happens in small, consistent actions. Choose habits that reinforce who you're becoming, not who you've been.

Example:

- The identity: *I am a leader.*

- The habit: Start the day by setting your top 3 priorities, lead one conversation, and make one tough decision.

4.Replace Old Beliefs, One by One

Every time an old, limiting belief surfaces, challenge it.

- *Is this belief absolutely true?*

- *Where did I learn it?*

- *What's a more empowering belief I can install instead?*

Your Operating System Is Always Either Strengthening or Weakening

There's no neutral. Every day, you're either becoming stronger, clearer, and more aligned or slipping into old defaults. The moment you stop choosing your thoughts, the world will choose them for you.

Own the Controls

Once you truly grasp that your identity, beliefs, and behaviours are yours to upgrade, and not the world's to dictate, you step out of the fog.

You stop reacting to life and start *shaping it.*

You stop wishing for better and start *choosing better.*

This is the shift that turns people from passive dreamers into conscious creators.

Key Takeaway:

You are not your circumstances. You are your operating system. And you have the power to rewrite it, update it, and design a life by choice, not chance.

Chapter 12:
The Power of Attention and Intention

If there's one thing I've learned, and re-learned, it's that **what you focus on expands**. The mind isn't just a storage device for memories and knowledge; it's a projector. It doesn't simply record life, it shapes it. The ancient mystics, modern neuroscientists, and philosophers alike have all pointed toward the same truth: **where your attention goes, your energy flows, and reality follows**.

Most people never question what their attention is doing day to day. It drifts, it fixates on problems, on judgments, on fears, and in doing so, it energises those very things. You don't attract what you want; you attract what you consistently think about, feel, and focus on.

When we set our **intention**, we give the mind a direction, like a compass needle finding north. Intention is the quiet but powerful declaration of 'this is who I am becoming, this is the reality I am creating.' It doesn't require shouting affirmations into the mirror for hours. It requires clarity, consistency, and congruence.

The laws of attraction, which many people misunderstand as a passive wish-list system, are actually grounded in this alignment of **thought, feeling, and focused action**. You don't just sit back and visualise your dream life; you hold that vision while moving toward it, while becoming the person that life would naturally deliver those outcomes to.

Consider this:

If your attention is on problems, you'll see more problems.

If your attention is on opportunity, you'll begin to notice ideas, people, and circumstances aligning to that frequency.

The mind works like a search engine; what you type into it is what it brings back to you.

The Energy of Intention

Intention isn't just about goals or outcomes. It's about the energy behind your actions. Two people can perform the same action, and one will succeed where the other fails because the **intention behind it carries more power**. Why? Because the universe, or if you prefer, the subconscious mind, responds more to **energy and emotion** than it does to logic.

A clear, heart-driven intention opens pathways. It turns chance encounters into pivotal moments. It makes setbacks feel like training rounds rather than defeats.

Reclaiming Control

Most of us have unintentionally surrendered control of our attention. Social media algorithms, fear-based news, and comparison culture hijack our focus and rewire our priorities. The antidote is **conscious awareness.**

You must take back the steering wheel of your mind.

Ask yourself throughout the day: *Where is my attention right now? Is this serving my intention or feeding distraction and limitation?*

If it's not serving you, redirect it. Not with guilt or force, but with quiet authority — the way a seasoned sailor adjusts the sails when the wind changes.

Living with Daily Intentionality

What if you woke up tomorrow and, before reaching for your phone or diving into the noise, you asked:

What is my intention for today? What energy do I want to carry into this day? What frequency am I going to broadcast into the world?

Do this enough times, and you'll notice the world responding differently. Not because the world changed, but because **you did.**

Attention + Intention = Creation.

This is one of the simplest, most profound formulas for reclaiming your life.

Chapter 13:
The Magnetic Pull of Intention

We've now peeled back many layers of who we are, how our programming was shaped, and the powerful internal forces at play within us. In this chapter, we lean into a force that's always been working for or against us, depending on how we use it. That force is **intention.**

Intention is more than a wish, more than a hopeful thought. It's a declaration of direction, a conscious alignment of thought, emotion, and action toward a chosen outcome. Where attention goes, energy flows, and where energy flows, outcomes begin to take form.

Think of the mind as a sculptor and your intention as the vision that guides the hand. Without a clear image of what you're creating, the sculptor's hand moves aimlessly. With a sharp, emotionally-charged intention, the mind begins to command your subconscious, your emotions, and even external opportunities toward that outcome.

The Law of Attraction in Motion

It's here that the **Law of Attraction** quietly but relentlessly weaves into our experience. Like attracts like. What you hold as a dominant thought and feeling in your inner world starts to shape your external world. It's not magic, it's the physics of consciousness. The vibration you emit through your thoughts, emotions, and actions calls forth experiences, people, and events that resonate with that same frequency.

If you constantly dwell in fear, life delivers confirming reasons to be afraid.

If you radiate an expectation of abundance, abundance starts to find its way to you.

This is why becoming aware of our internal operating system, as we covered in earlier chapters, is crucial. It is so because whether you're aware of it or not, you're always manifesting, but are you manifesting what you want, or what you fear?

Setting Intentions, Not Just Goals

Goals are great, but intentions are goals infused with energy and presence. A goal is "I want to be financially free."

An intention is **"I live every day taking aligned action toward freedom, feeling abundant, powerful, and grateful now."**

Notice the difference?

An intention claims it in the present and carries emotion. That emotional charge is what fuels the manifestation process.

Emotion is energy in motion.

The stronger and more genuine the emotion behind an intention, the faster it magnetises corresponding circumstances.

An Exercise in Conscious Intention

I encourage you to pause right now, close your eyes, and ask yourself:

- *What is it I truly desire right now?*

- *Why do I want it?*

- *How will it feel when I have it?*

Now — don't just think about it. Feel it. Embody it as if it's already real. The mind cannot tell the difference between what's vividly imagined with emotion and what's physically experienced.

Hold this state for a minute or two. Do this daily. Watch how your perception begins to shift, how new ideas arrive, how chance encounters happen. These are not coincidences; they're confirmations of your new alignment.

Beware the Undermining Thought

Intentions work best when they're clear and unpolluted by contradiction. Saying "I want to build a thriving business" while secretly thinking "but I'll probably fail like last time" is like driving with one foot on the accelerator and one on the brake.

Clean up the internal dialogue.

Replace "I'm not good enough" with **"I'm learning, growing, and capable."**

Replace "I'll probably fail" with **"I'm committed to succeeding, and every experience grows me stronger."**

This isn't naive optimism, it's mental discipline, and it's how all high performers operate.

The Universe Responds to Clarity

You don't have to know *how* it will happen.

You just need to be clear on *what* and *why*, stay emotionally aligned with it, and trust the process.

Life rearranges itself around your dominant intentions.

When you start living on purpose, with conscious intentions, you shift from being a passenger in life to its deliberate architect.

Chapter 14:
Flow and Alignment

Throughout this book, we've explored how our thoughts, beliefs, emotions, and actions shape the lives we lead. But to truly create lasting, meaningful change, it's time we step back and see the bigger picture, to understand that everything in existence operates within a vast, moving flow of energy. And whether we realise it or not, we're part of that flow every moment of our lives.

The universe isn't a collection of static, disconnected events. It's a living, breathing force in constant motion. Like a current in a river or the rise and fall of a tide, energy moves, expands, and contracts. It carries people, opportunities, and outcomes with it. And the truth is, we're either moving with it or against it.

When You're Out of Flow

We often get caught in repeating cycles of frustration, doubt, fear, and indecision because we've stepped out of alignment with that natural current. When you operate from negative emotions and limiting beliefs, you effectively block yourself off from what's available to you. You stop hearing the quiet guidance of your intuition. You overlook opportunities. You cling to control and force outcomes, and as a result, life feels like an uphill battle.

This isn't bad luck or some external force working against you. It's simply what happens when we disrupt our own connection to the natural rhythm of life. And like we've touched on in earlier chapters — our identity, thoughts, emotions, and actions either create alignment or resistance. Left unchecked, that resistance piles up over time, becoming our default operating state.

Moving Into Alignment

The goal isn't to control life's flow — it's to learn how to move with it, to tune your internal world in a way that allows you to travel effortlessly with the current. When you do this, life begins to unfold more naturally. You'll notice things fall into place with less effort. You'll feel clearer, calmer, and more decisive. Doors open. People appear. Ideas arrive at the perfect time.

This alignment isn't achieved by accident. It's a practice — a daily awareness of how you're showing up internally and how you're responding to the world around you. It's about recognising when you've slipped into old patterns and gently guiding yourself back onto your path.

The Foundation of Flow

There are four essential forces that bring us back into alignment with the energy of life:

1. **Presence**

Most of our suffering comes from living in the past or worrying about the future. When we anchor ourselves in the present moment, we reconnect with what's real. From this space, we become aware of the subtle guidance available to us, the opportunities in front of us, and the decisions that truly matter.

2. Clear Intentions

The clearer you are on what you want, the easier it becomes to notice opportunities that align with it. When your intentions are scattered or half-hearted, you send mixed signals to yourself and to the world around you. Clarity isn't about controlling every detail; it's about knowing the kind of life you want to live and the person you choose to become.

3. Emotional Alignment

Your emotional state either lifts you into alignment or drags you into resistance. When you prioritise emotions like gratitude, peace, curiosity, and optimism, you naturally elevate your experience and invite better outcomes. This isn't about pretending to be happy all the time; it's about consciously choosing states that support the life you want.

4. Inspired Action

Moving with the flow of life still requires action. The difference is, instead of forcing outcomes or chasing validation, you take steps from a place of clarity and trust.

Inspired actions feel purposeful, even if they stretch your comfort zone. They come with a sense of internal "knowing" rather than external pressure.

Why So Many Stay Stuck

Most people never realise they're out of flow because resistance has become normal. They wake up carrying yesterday's fears, beliefs, and emotional baggage, and unknowingly repeat the same decisions that keep them stuck. It's not until you slow down, tune in, and take an honest look at your patterns that you'll see how often you've been swimming against the current.

That's why I encourage you now to revisit the earlier chapters of this book. The wisdom you uncover the second time through will be different. You'll read it with fresh eyes. As you grow, new layers of understanding reveal themselves. That's how real transformation works: it's a cycle of learning, applying, reflecting, and realigning.

Your Six-Week Realignment Plan

To help you move from theory into practice, here's a simple, effective plan you can start right now. Over the next six weeks, you'll address the key areas of your internal world, one layer at a time.

Week	Focus Area	What to Do
1	Identity Check	Journal: Who am I becoming? vs Who have I been?
2	Belief Audit	Choose one limiting belief and consciously replace it
3	Emotional Calibration	Track your dominant emotions daily; introduce gratitude
4	Intention Strengthening	Spend 5 minutes visualising your ideal outcomes each day
5	Inspired Action Integration	Pick 3 bold, meaningful actions and commit to them
6	Flow Check & Reflection	Notice where life feels easier or heavier; adjust accordingly

Use this plan not as a rigid checklist, but as a living guide. Some weeks you'll feel on fire. Other weeks, you might struggle. Both are part of the process. What matters is your willingness to stay engaged.

Surrender Is Not Giving Up

One of the most powerful shifts you can make is to let go of needing to control every detail. This doesn't mean becoming passive or indifferent. It means trusting that life will meet you halfway when you meet yourself fully. When you align your identity, beliefs, emotions, intentions, and actions with what you truly want — and stay open to how it arrives — life begins to flow through you, not against you.

You stop chasing. You stop forcing. You start allowing.

The Shift from Resistance to Power

As you practice this, you'll notice subtle yet profound changes:

- Fear softens into curiosity

- Stress transforms into motivation

- Doubt becomes insight

- Uncertainty turns into opportunity

That's the real work. Not to avoid discomfort, but to use it as a signal, a reminder to come back into alignment.

Key Message:

The universe moves in a natural flow, and you have the choice every day to move with it or against it. Alignment is not luck; it's built through presence, clarity, emotional mastery, and intentional action. And when you live from this place, life has a beautiful way of carrying you exactly where you're meant to be.

Chapter 15 - The 8 Powers of the Mind

Your operating toolkit for navigating life, upgrading your mindset, and staying aligned with your highest self.

Withdraw

To withdraw is not to run away — it's to reclaim control.

It means pulling your emotions out of a situation before it consumes your energy.

We aren't withdrawing from life, but from negativity, pointless arguments, toxic energy, or chaotic environments.

Example:

Imagine someone cuts you off in traffic, flipping you off as they speed away. Your immediate reaction might be to shout, curse, or chase them down mentally for the next 20 minutes. But if you have the power to withdraw, you recognise *this isn't my battle*, take a deep breath, and pull your energy away. You leave the emotion behind and stay aligned.

Another example is during heated family arguments. It takes strength not to add fuel to a fire you have no reason to burn in. Withdraw inwardly, centre yourself, and respond later, if at all, from a place of peace.

Power Move:

Withdrawal allows you to pause, reset your energy, and operate with wisdom instead of impulse.

Co-Operate

To co-operate is to work together for a higher outcome.

It's understanding that life is a collaborative process. Even the most 'independent' person depends on others every day.

Analogy:

Picture catching a flight. You couldn't afford the entire plane, fuel, or maintenance alone.

But by co-operating, you buy your seat, others buy theirs, and suddenly you're soaring through the sky together. Behind that flight is a team of pilots, engineers, air traffic controllers, baggage handlers, catering staff, and manufacturers.

Co-operation makes the impossible possible.

Power Move:

When you choose to co-operate instead of compete, you multiply potential outcomes, strengthen relationships, and become a magnet for support.

Face

Facing things head-on is how we grow.

The more we avoid, the more life mirrors our avoidance back at us. Issues don't disappear; they wait for us, often in bigger and heavier forms.

Example:

Imagine avoiding a difficult conversation with a business partner or spouse. You know it's uncomfortable, so you delay it. But avoidance builds tension and resentment. When you finally face it, with calm, clarity, and courage, you release the blockage and the growth begins.

Power Move:

Every time you face what you fear or avoid, you shrink the shadow it casts over your life.

Judge

Judging is often misunderstood. The power lies in using it wisely.

We're constantly judging, but the key is to judge *without prejudice*. It means making clear, fair, conscious decisions about what's right for you, without diminishing others.

Example:

You discriminate between an apple and an orange, not because one is better, but because they serve different needs. In life, you must discern between opportunity and distraction, truth and illusion, healthy company and harmful influence.

Power Move:

Healthy judgment helps you make clear decisions, protect your energy, and navigate life without getting lost in others' chaos.

Pack Up

There's wisdom in knowing when something is done.

Unlike withdrawal, which is momentary, *pack up* means to emotionally and mentally close a chapter.

Example:

You've done your best in a relationship, job, or project, but it's no longer serving you. The lesson's complete. Rather than clinging out of fear or habit, you gracefully pack up your emotional investment and move on, creating space for new energy.

Power Move:

Knowing when to let go is a master skill. Clinging slows you down; closing frees you.

Tolerate

Tolerance isn't weakness, it's wisdom.

It means having the patience and understanding to see that people are carrying their own pain and stories.

Example:

A colleague snaps at you during a meeting. Instead of reacting, you pause and think, *They must be carrying something heavier than they're showing.* That insight stops you from getting dragged into unnecessary negativity.

Power Move:

Tolerance keeps your energy intact in a world full of triggers.

Adjust

Life won't adjust to you; you must adjust to life.

It means recognising when the environment changes and moving with it, not against it.

Example:

You walk into a room expecting formality, but it's relaxed and casual. Rather than clinging to expectations, you adjust, blending with the room's vibe while remaining yourself.

In business, this skill is invaluable. Markets change, people change, opportunities shift, and those who adjust thrive.

Power Move:

Adjustment lets you stay relevant, resilient, and at peace in any environment.

Discriminate

Discrimination here means clear separation, knowing what belongs to you, and what doesn't.

Separating truth from illusion, positive influence from negative, wisdom from noise.

Example:

You're bombarded with opinions: what to believe, buy, fear, chase. The power of discrimination helps you sort through this clutter and act in alignment with your truth.

Power Move:

Discrimination sharpens your intuition, keeps your vision clear, and prevents you from being led by the blind.

Final Thought on the 8 Powers

These 8 Powers aren't abstract theories — they're practical, usable tools. Think of them like mental muscles. The more you practice them, the stronger your inner operating system becomes.

By consciously calling on these Powers throughout your day, when challenges arise, conversations turn tense, or opportunities appear, you begin reprogramming your mind. You shift from reactive to proactive. From impulsive to intentional. From powerless to powerful.

This is how you build *Mind, the Original AI,* into your daily operating system.

Chapter 16:
The Beginning of the Rest of Your Life

As we arrive at the final pages of this book, I want you to take a breath and acknowledge something important, you made it here for a reason.

Somewhere deep within you, perhaps even beyond what you fully understand right now, was a pull. A quiet nudge. A sense that you were meant to reconnect with something more. And not just to learn it, but to live it.

This book was never about giving you answers you didn't already possess. It was about helping you remember.

We were born into this world with power. Love. Peace. Courage. Joy. Truth. These weren't learned behaviours, they were our original settings. Life, through its trials and hurts, gradually layered over them with fear, limitation, and self-doubt. We internalised the opinions of others, misinterpreted failures as evidence of our worth, and slowly forgot who we really are.

But you've now taken steps to peel those layers back.

You've looked at how identity is built. How your subconscious mind, like fertile soil, grows whatever seeds you consistently plant. How your environment, words, and thoughts either support your potential or suffocate it. How operating from a negative state keeps you cycling in patterns that feel like fate but are nothing more than the result of unconscious alignment with the wrong energy.

And most importantly, you've learned that *you can choose differently.*

The Universe Moves For You, When You Move For Yourself

Everything is energy. Every thought, every word, every action sends out a frequency. The universe, this constantly moving, infinitely intelligent energy field, isn't keeping score of your failures. It isn't punishing you for mistakes. It simply responds to what you consistently *are.*

If you carry fear, you'll meet more reasons to be afraid.

If you move with gratitude, you'll find more to be grateful for.

If you pursue growth with faith and conviction, life will open doors you never saw coming.

The laws that govern this aren't superstition or wishful thinking. They are cause and effect. You already live by them, whether you're conscious of it or not.

The difference now is that you can operate deliberately.

The Map Forward

Before you set this book down, I want to offer you a simple but powerful plan to begin living aligned with what you truly want:

1. Reconnect with Your Original Powers

Each morning, remind yourself: *I was born with love, courage, peace, joy, and truth. Today I will honour them.*

2. Choose the Higher Operating State

Notice when you're moving in sadness, fear, lies, or chaos. Name it. Then choose differently. Ask: *What would courage do right now? What would peace say?*

3. Set Clear Intentions Daily

Not vague hopes, clear, affirmative intentions. *I will speak my truth today. I will welcome the opportunity. I will show up as my highest self.*

4. Surround Yourself Intentionally

Environments shape outcomes. Audit your circle. Your habits. Your media. Choose what amplifies your light.

5. Act Boldly, Even When Fear Kicks In

The aim isn't to eliminate fear, it's to move in spite of it. Courage is action with heart racing and hands trembling.

6. Believe, Even Before Evidence Arrives

The universe responds to alignment, not desperation. Trust the unseen, hold your vision, and live as though it's already unfolding.

Your New Story Begins Now

I want you to know something: no matter where you've been, what mistakes you've made, or what limitations you've carried, you are *one decision away* from a different life.

Not because it's easy. Not because it's guaranteed. But because the power to redirect your story never left you.

We were born aligned with possibility. Life dimmed that flame. This book was your reminder to reignite it.

Now, reread the chapters as many times as you need. Reflect on the exercises. Sit with the uncomfortable truths. And then? Move.

Because the only thing standing between you and the life you were designed for is the story you choose to believe from this point forward.

And I hope, with everything in me, that you choose wisely.

This isn't the end. It's the beginning. Let's get to work.

Final Reflection:
Return to the Source

By now, you'll have realised something important.

The battle was never out there. It was always in here, in the mind.

And once you claim control over your inner world, your outer world cannot help but change.

You've learned about energy, thought cycles, habit loops, old programs, and the power of your conscious mind. You've looked back at your old stories and glimpsed a future no longer limited by them. You've been reminded of the original qualities you were born with: peace, courage, happiness, love, and truth.

And you've remembered that the most powerful intelligence you'll ever possess isn't an app or a piece of technology.

It's your mind. The Original AI.

The universe is constantly moving, expanding, and offering you new chances to align. The question is no longer whether life will keep coming at you; it's whether you'll flow with it or fight against it.

This is your call to flow.

When you find yourself slipping back into old thoughts, reread these pages. When doubt creeps in, remind yourself of the energy you are and the power you hold. And when life seems chaotic, remember that the only thing you truly control is the program you choose to run.

You are the coder. You are the operator. You are the master.

And as you move forward, know this:

You don't need to seek permission to live an extraordinary life. You were built for it.

Level up, and see you on the next level.

Thomas Lashan

www.ingramcontent.com/pod-product-compliance
Lightning Source LLC
Chambersburg PA
CBHW031448120626
46545CB00006B/2616